NARCISSISTIC ABUSE RECOVERY

UNDERSTANDING NARCISSISM AND RECOVERING FROM NARCISSISTIC ABUSE

© Copyright 2018 by _____ - All rights reserved.

The following eBook is reproduced below with the goal of providing information that is as accurate and reliable as possible. Regardless, purchasing this eBook can be seen as consent to the fact that both the publisher and the author of this book are in no way experts on the topics discussed within and that any recommendations or suggestions that are made herein are for entertainment purposes only. Professionals should be consulted as needed prior to undertaking any of the action endorsed herein.

This declaration is deemed fair and valid by both the American Bar Association and the Committee of Publishers Association and is legally binding throughout the United States.

Furthermore, the transmission, duplication or reproduction of any of the following work including specific information will be considered an illegal act irrespective of if it is done electronically or in print. This extends to creating a secondary or tertiary copy of the work or a recorded copy and is only allowed with an expressed written consent from the Publisher. All additional rights reserved.

The information in the following pages is broadly considered to be truthful and accurate account of facts,and as such any inattention, use or misuse of the information in question by the reader will render any resulting actions solely under their purview. There are no scenarios in which the publisher or the original author of this work can be in any fashion deemed liable for any hardship or damages that may befall them after undertaking information described herein.

Additionally, the information in the following pages is intended only for informational purposes and should thus be thought of as universal. As befitting its nature, it is presented without assurance regarding its prolonged validity or interim quality. Trademarks that are mentioned are done without written consent and can in no way be considered an endorsement from the trademark holder.

Table of Contents

Introduction i

Chapter 1: UnderstandingNarcissism 1

Chapter 2: What Makes Up Narcissistic Personality Disorder 17

Chapter 3: Narcissists in Relationships 51

Chapter 4: Narcissism and Attachment Theory 65

Chapter 5: How to Spot Narcissists 84

Chapter 6: First Steps of Recovery from Narcissistic abuse 101

Chapter 7: Moving on from Narcissistic Abuse 123

Chapter 8: Emotional Self-Care Practices forNarcissistic Abuse Recovery 138

Conclusion 149

Introduction

Narcissism has become popularized through popular media outlets in the form of film, articles or various personalities. The image of the narcissist is one who is attractive, successful and aloof. They also tend to care only about themselves and are ruthless. From the descriptions provided by the media, the only thing which is true is their key attribute of only caring about themselves. Narcissists account for about 6 percent of the population, and they come from all walks of life. They might be your friend, neighbor, romantic partner, colleague, boss or even family member. As such, they could be closer to you in life than you might think and this should jog your assessment of relationships you are in because it is quite hard for someone to realize they have such a person in their lives. In narcissistic abuse recovery, you will have to shed the mentality that people are inherently good because the typical narcissist is far from that. They have a disorder which places them at the center of their world. They do not have a moral control or a functioning superego as it were. Narcissists approach can be likened to that of a vampire. It sees everything else as insignificant or food.

A narcissist views a potential target in the same way a predator views prey. They get in your life and force you to isolate through psychological manipulation,and then they start to feed off your feelings through a cycle of neglect, abuse,and reinvigoration. The narcissist believes that everyone else is there to serve them. So, when you are in the recovery process, you need to come to terms with the horror of the situation so that it becomes imperative to detach rather than do conflict resolution. This book delves not only into the nature of the narcissist and how they think but also the recovery process which will require self-healing techniques that are outlined throughout the book. Self-love, in this case, includes eating the right things and following a schedule that will make you better able to control your thought process. It is quite easy for an emotionally injured person to fall back into the traps set by their abusers or to continually obsess. The basis of self-healing is to make sure that you do not have to go back to that life. A lot of these recovery approaches are based on methods used in post-traumatic treatment so the level of trauma can be severe and you may have to contact professional help if you feel that it would be necessary. Abuse recovery needs to be thought of as a lifestyle as well. It is not a one-time thing that will be practiced when you have attacks. Think of it as a fresh start that can assist you on the path of healing.

Chapter 1: Understanding Narcissism

Narcissism as a concept refers to self-adoration and aloofness. It has been the subject of concern in psychology and in social circles. In mythology, Narcissus a Greek character during the 8th century falls in love with his image and is frustrated because it is not possible to unite with his object of affection and pines away, eventually dying. It is said that the gods sentenced Narcissus to a life that did not have human love. He fell in love with his own reflection in a pool of water and then died from apparent neglect from the object of his affections.

In 1898, Ellis instituted the term known as narcissism to apply to autoerotic behavior, which is a sexual depravity that worries the individual taking himself as a sexual object. Disregarding its ensuing changing utilize, the term held ramifications of a positive inclination toward the self-removed from extent. It was Freud that gave narcissism a place over the span of human sexual improvement as a component of his hypothesis concerning libido. Making the presumption that an individual has a settled measure of libido available to him the focal part of the hypothesis was libidinal cathexis regarding the matter is object love and libidinal cathexis on the self as narcissism. The Freudian phase of essential narcissism started at the time that the individual had simple subject mindfulness. The libido in essential narcissism is put resources into the portrayal of the self. As the ego limits were made, libidinal cathexis relating the object came to fruition and some libido remaining appended to the self as leftover methods for essential narcissism.

This conceptualization of narcissism was presently the reason for the ego perfect which was perceived as the store of remainders of puerile narcissism. The advancing thoughts concerning narcissism continued with his later portrayal of a narcissistic libidinal write described by self-certainty and at affectedness at the extraordinary. Narcissistic libido at that point turned into the premise of self-esteem.Now, some people maybe narcissistic,but they do not have a mental illness. When thinking of them, you might picture an individual that has an inflated sense of ego, is arrogance and has to be right all of the time. To be diagnosed with what has come to be known as the Narcissistic

Personality Disorder or NPD, that individual has to show elements of grandiosity to a level of fantasy. They also have to lack any form of empathy. Some of the symptoms include dreams of unlimited power, belief that they are unique and special and can only be understood by people of the same status. They also need an excessive amount of admiration and affirmation. They envy others or believe they are jealous of their supposed achievements and they expect unreasonable treatment. There are various types such as the closet narcissists have been identified as those who have a deflated inadequate self-perception and a sense of depression and inner emptiness. They could be shy, humble or anxious because their emotional investment is in the idealized other and that is indirectly gratifying.

The more aggressive type is malignant narcissists who are cruel and vindictive at any time they feel threatened or do not get what they want.

Heinz Kohut had the observation that his narcissistic patients suffered a lot of alienation, powerlessness, and lack of meaning. Beneath the narcissistic façade, they did not have the right internal structures to maintain a form of cohesiveness, stability and positive self-imageto give the right identity. Narcissists have been found to not be certain concerning the boundaries that exist between others and themselves, and so they may vacillate between the dissociated versions of inferiority and inflation. The self, when divided by shame, is built on superior acting, the inferior and the devalued self. When the devalued self is in an inferior designation, then shame can manifest through the idealization of others.

At the time that the individual is in the right position defending against shame, then the grandiose self may align with the inner critic and then devalue others through the means of projection.

Even though some people fluctuate when in these positions, the aggressive and introverted narcissists are basically more static in their superior and inferior positions irrespective of the reality, and this could make them pathological. Arrogance, withdrawal, denial, envy and contempt or projections are some of the common defenses which may have towards shame. The narcissists also have a tendency for defending against fragmentation and shame through feeling special using idealizing or identifying with special people. In the home situation, you might find that narcissists are very different as compared to the persona they give to the public. They can privately denigrate the individual that they had been entertaining at an earlier time. After the first pleasantries and romance with a partner, they expect appreciation of the way they are special and particular responses through demands or criticism to manage their internal environment and protect against high sensitivity when it comes to humiliation and shame. Relations can revolve around them, and they may experience their partners as an extension of themselves.

Narcissists usually face the psychological challenge of how to keep being in love with themselves and feel like they are special people even in the face of evident failure. For example, Hitler at the time that he sensed defeat was imminent, and the Allies were closing in on Berlin, however, that instance ended in suicide. Though, many true narcissists are not capable of taking their own lives to prove the concept of self-love. One approach would be to use others as pawns in the grand scheme of deception. If one is able to execute this will by convincing yourself and others that you are as good as you think, then it is possible to win the game of self-admiration. The Narcissists can brag about their achievements and focus on physical appearance and material goods displaying status or always turn the conversation to being about them. They may also surround themselves with individuals that are lower in status and look up to them. Because they may not value warm or caring forms of relationships,they might do this without a lot of concern for other individuals usually manipulating and exploiting individuals and viewing others as tools so that they can feel good about their achievements.

Researchers have detailed these as efforts to attain some form of self-admiration. The narcissist has a lot of time spent on the regulation of their social relationships to maximize self-admiration. If or when it works, the narcissist then feels euphoric and has a sense of pride,but when it does not, they are likely to lash out with blame and rage at their underlings or the people who are closest to them at the time. An example, in this case, would be a likable character that on camera is charming,however, in the private setting they are not hospitable and quite unbearable to be around.

There are different myths that surround the condition though. When you ask around about narcissism, there are a lot of interesting suppositions. The first is that narcissism is just really high self-esteem. According to Freud Narcissism did form the basis that came to be known as the ego in the human mind which is where people develop self-worth, but this was at the elementary level. Narcissists do have high self-worth, and in fact, many of the approaches used to increase esteem could lead to a greater level of narcissism. However, the two are quite different. Narcissists for one think they think, look and talk better than others though they do not have a counterbalance of any form of morality or conscience. One can imagine from the Freudian concepts, an ego without a superego. Narcissists do not necessarily brag they are the nicest or thoughtful individuals in the world though they like to claim they are winners or they are the best looking. People who just have high self-esteem also have a positive view of themselves though they also tend to view themselves as having a conscience or having a sense of morality. That is the one reason narcissists do not have perspective as close relationships keep the ego in check. They are missing the piece that relates to caring for others,and that is the reason why their self-admiration can go out of control.

The other myth is that narcissists tend to be individuals of a higher class in terms of beauty, finances or social ability. It would be easier for a person to be a narcissist if they actually had something to back it up or they were very talented at something. However, there is not a lot of evidence that narcissists happen to be any better on average. There are studies which have shown that narcissists typically do not score any better when it comes to objective IQ testing, and there are other tests that did not find any correlation between performance and narcissism on a test concerning general knowledge. Studies linked to creativity have come up with mixed results on the matter with one of them coming up with a positive correlation and another having zero links. It would then make sense that narcissists are generally not different from the rest of the people. They also seem to not be any better looking. There has been research which rated headshots from a sample of individuals. The results were that the narcissists were not found to be any more attractive as compared to others even in the event they thought they were much better looking. What they are good at apparently is being able to pick out pictures that are flattering concerning the way they look.

Finally, there is a myth that narcissists happen to be insecure. The basis of the theory is narcissists believe they do not deserve companionship or happiness and so they hate themselves deep down. The theory contends that their self-importance is something they use as misdirect to cover issues which are deep-seated about them. According to the psychodynamic theory, narcissism is related as a defense against empty or hidden low self-esteem and a deep sense of shame. At times psychologists designate this as the mask model because it implied that narcissism is a mask that hides low self-worth.

The argument is seductive considering its convenience that then allows one to write off narcissistic individuals as souls that are flawed and just need to learn to love themselves enough. You can believe that narcissists are actually suffering even though they may seem happy or satisfied with themselves. That perspective coincides with psychodynamic elaborations concerning behavior where the conscious and unconscious oppose each other.

A lot of the information that is there concerning narcissism is based according to the ideology that a narcissist underneath is suffering from low self-worth. In fact, there are online sites which claim to have expertise on the subject that claim narcissists actually have low self-esteem and have a sense of insecurity around other individuals. It is this insecure feeling that would lead to a grandiose image of being perfect in some ways. For example, there is the example that Paris Hilton seems confident but that she is in fact insecure. There is a mass perspective that insecurity is the crucial difference between self-confidence and narcissism. It is a way to have one's cake and eat it. The fact is there is no evidence currently that the extraverted narcissist actually has a low sense of self-esteem. They like themselves the way they are and much more than the common person. Adults that rate high when it comes to the narcissism scale usually also score highly on self-worth ratings. The most common measure of self-confidence has items including 'I feel that I have many good qualities.' Someone that thought he was entitled to the best would probably find little to disagree with. To the narcissists, these self-esteem things sound like a pale shadow of their own significance.

Chapter 2: What Makes Up Narcissistic Personality Disorder

Source: https://blogs.psychcentral.com/narcissism-decoded/2017/06/the-narcissists-alphabet/

A narcissistic personality disorder may cause some issues in different areas of life like work, relationships, school or even in the financial arena. The people that suffer from this condition are generally unhappy and disappointed when they are not issued with the special admiration or favors they are sure they deserve. They could find their relationships to be unfulfilling,and other individuals may not enjoy the feeling of being around such characters. The signs and symptoms have already been covered though they entail a great sense of entitlement and a high self-esteem. There is also exaggerated achievements and talents, monopolization of conversations and special favors not to mention unquestioning compliance with expectations. They are also likely not to have an easy time receiving criticism for their behavior or performance in different aspects. They have issues regulating their emotions and experience a lot of trouble adapting to changing situations or dealing with high stress. This is probably due to the fact, they are perfectionists and control freaks so unfamiliar environments are not their forte.

The people that have NPD as it is called may not want to believe that anything may be wrong which is why they are not likely to seek treatment. When they seek treatment, the probability is it is for symptoms related to drug, alcohol usage or for other mental issues but not that. The trouble with NPD is it gives the perception of an insult to their self-esteem,and this makes it difficult to follow through and accept treatment because according to them, they do not have a problem in the first place. If you recognize aspects of your personality are corresponding to the ones laid for narcissistic personality disorder,itwill behoove you to reach out to a trusted mental health provider.

A narcissistic personality disorder may affect more of the males as compared to the females though,andusually, it starts during the teens or during the early parts of adulthood. One needs to keep in mind however that some of the children may show characteristics of narcissism, this could just be typical concerning their age,and it does not mean that they will proceed to the full stage development of narcissistic personality disorder. Even though the cause is not yet fully pinned down, a lot of researchers are of the belief that when it comes to biologically vulnerable children, the parenting styles that tend to be more on the overprotective side or neglectful could have a negative effect.

Genetic Causes

Experiences during childhood are known to be significant towards the development of this disorder. There are genetic markings which contribute and initiate a high vulnerability for the problem, in the same way, there would be for other mental illness types. Without a high genetic predisposition when it comes to narcissism, then NPD is not likely to develop unless there are environmental agents which are uncharacteristically strong and help to initiate such situations. The question of genetics and personality issues, in general, has been thoroughly studied in the recent times for some disorders more than others, but there has been a consistent connection illustrated between narcissistic attributes and factors that can be inherited. The effect is not exactly overwhelming, but it would be strong enough to play a big role in the development of the disorder.

As such, there is estimation that about 6 percent of the American population has a narcissistic personality disorder that happens to be more common in men as well and has roots that begin in childhood. The nature of the way it is oriented as a disorder means the individual is extremely resistant to any treatment. This severe illness leads the individuals to create chaos as they create a lot of harm to others on a sociological level. Before considering how demands for support of ego and desires, there should be an analysis of pertinent normal child development. Small children for one are naturally selfish as a normal part of their development in which they work to have their needs considered and met.

Until this point, they are not able to understand the needs and desires of others and how it relates to their own in the scheme of things. As teens, the kids typically become self-centered as they continue to struggle for self-identity. As opposed to self-centeredness that generally decreases, children should then start to develop healthy and long-lasting esteem to protect and care for others while still caring about themselves. This is to deviate from dangerous influences and to stay connected to the family and the society as a whole. Healthy levels of esteem are indicative that the child believes they are loved and are worthy of their societal level, so they do not deserve to be mistreated or have a thick skin for it. More importantly, they start to get a feel for themselves what it should be like to treat others and what it entails to live adequately within the communal setting. Now, unfortunately, the narcissism that is in particular children will not be detected typically as children are expected to act in a self-centered manner. After all, one might say they are just acting in their own self-interest or that they do not know any better. Considering the discipline levels of the current society, the levels of empathy are steadily falling in children,and so it is getting quite hard to tell which an issue with morality is and what a danger sign is for a future narcissist.

The typical childhood self-centeredness has to change to pave the way for mental stability when the child starts to become an adult. To grow up able to function in the right way in families, the kids have to gradually gain the stability to see the perspectives of others and empathy as concerns the suffering of other people. Healthy children should then show a gradual development in this sector and show sincere signs of caring about the wellbeing of others. Now developing a sense of empathy while a child is growing up is a big warning sign of a serious personality issue as an adult and is one of the warning signs for narcissism in the adult stages. The question though is whether the children that develop into narcissists and showed the warning signs of morality and empathy early on were born with it or the environment was a factor early on from the time they were born.

In 2008 there was a study carried out in Scandinavia which considered 3000 nonidentical twins and genetic factors were found to have a 25 percent influence on the development of narcissistic traits in the participants of the study. Environmental influences covered the remaining percentage of course. There was another study that was done in Asia recently on two particular attributes for NPD which was a sense of entitlement and feelings of being grandiose. The study showed there was an inheritance factor of 23 percent for feelings of grandiosity and 35 percent for entitlement. That means the children had a 35 chance of having entitlement and a lower chance of having feelings of grandiosity which is the stronger narcissistic trait. This confirms the contributions of genetic effects even when the narcissistic symptoms are analyzed when in isolation.

There was another study done by Lindsey in 2007 where narcissism, as measured by a standardized test, became a common inherited trait. In the study,175 volunteer twin pairs were gotten from the general population. Each of them did a questionnaire which was an assessment of eighteen characteristics of a personality disorder. The authors estimated the heritability for each of the characteristics through standard methodology then giving estimates concerning the relative contribution of genetic causation. Narcissism, in this case, was found to have the highest level of heritability,and this means the trait is the identical twins was influenced a lot by genetics. When it came to the other seventeen attributes, only four of them were found to be statistically significant such as identity problems, contrarianism, and callousness.

Similarly, advances made in technology such as brain imaging has proven that the brains of the ones suffering from issues like NPD, BPD, and Antisocial Personality Disorder which happen to be in the same cluster are not exactly functioning in the right manner. The activity levels when it comes to the brains of those suffering from the condition are said to be abnormal. Research done on cluster B type of personality disorders has also confirmed a lot of physiological brain dysfunction in two of the four cluster B problems. The reason why the brain is not functioning as it should is not yet known though. There is not a lot of research which has been done regarding this approach on NPD because most narcissists do not usually admit to having any problems unless they are forced to do so by their families or by the society. In fact, you might find that most available narcissists are those who are incarcerated for crimes done due to their condition. Additional research on conditions within the same spectrum has shown that these personality disorders have a rate of appearance in offspring at 68%. That would mean two-thirds of the children of the people that have issues with narcissism may also have it themselves. Overall the fact that brain imaging shows that people with this cluster B issues are quite different from the images of normal brain patterns shows that genetics does have a stake in the development of narcissistic personality disorder. These brain function patterns would not be influenced by environmental factors to become a certain way unless, through hard trauma, drugs or disease but these are farfetched reasons. This is not to say that environmental causes do not have a stake in creating narcissistic personality issues, but the genetics lay the foundation for these types of individuals. The brain functions of NPD patients are already wired in a certain way. It is the environmental factors which then capitalize on the already sowed potential to bring out these types of people in the society.

Environmental Factors

Source: http://www.minddisorders.com/Kau-Nu/Narcissistic-personality-disorder.html

When we are born, we are basically the sum of our genes. Mental illness cannot be analyzed without considering the brain, and the brain cannot be considered without analyzing the genetic structure. As such, any explanation concerning mental life that leaves out genetic makeup and neurophysiology is not there. Such theories are nothing but literary narratives. It is true that single genes rare account for particular behavior or traits. A group of coordinated genetic material is needed to explain even the smallest human attribute. It would appear reasonable to have the assumption that the narcissist is typically born with a propensity to develop NPD. These may be triggered by trauma and abuse at the time of the formative years when they are children or during the time they are in the teen years. By abuse, this refers to a spectrum of behaviors that objectifies the child and the treats it as an extension of the parent or a tool. Dotting behavior on the child may be as much a trigger as would starve or beating the child. The abuse can also be given out by peers or even other adult role models.

In the assessment of environmental factors that are responsible for the onset of mental problems, a lot of the focus is usually on the experiences of the person when they were a child. These set the tone and the template going forward for future mental processes and the development of their personality. Parenting styles and family dynamics particularly are significant to the emotional and psychological well-being, and it is the latter factor especially that would be decisive in the onset of narcissistic personality disorder during the time of adulthood.

Classical clinical theories on the origins of the disorder have also emphasized on the role of the environment especially when it comes to parenting behavior. It is this theorizing which has become part of the basis as concerns empirical research on the matter.

Clinical theorizing concerning narcissism and how it came to be can be traced to Freud, and the contemporary theories came from object relation enthusiasts such as Kohut and Kernberg. Now there may have been disagreements among the theorists concerning different issues, but the clinicians argue that the interactions of the child with parents are critical when it comes to the functional development of the way that child considers themselves and to whether the child is going to manifest a form of narcissism. When it comes to the source of self-identity in NPD, the focus placed on the parents.

Object relations

Even though psychodynamic and object relations theorists, for the most part, differ on the idea of narcissism when it comes and the specific sorts of child-rearing that are to blame, there is a concession to two things. For one, the theorists are of the possibility that early connections between the mother and child are huge towards the assurance of the nature and the levels of narcissism inside the child. Evidently, the cooperation occurring between the first and the second long periods of life are very basic to this improvement procedure even though ongoing discourses have recognized the dynamic and right now progressing nature as concerns the advancement of narcissism.

The other thing is theorists appear to concur that the intentions of the patent, when contrasted with that of the child, appear to be exceptionally prescient of the method of child-rearing that is being utilized and the level and the levels of narcissism that the child will show. Obviously, the motivational object relations viewpoint notes parental conduct is driven by contending intention frameworks. That would show that viable child rearing is a portrayal of a blend of two frameworks which is tipped toward the child-centered framework. Broken child rearing then again may control towards a child that is narcissistic,and it is generally coordinated without anyone else's input center.

The object relations approach veers on the subject of how self-center means broken child rearing. Obviously, self-centered child rearing is portrayed as either careless,or it is enmeshed thus either sort of child rearing may prompt narcissism. Be that as it may, narrow-minded guardians tend to put the child on a platform as the desire for magnificence for the family. The child-rearing at that point tends to be hyper requesting of the child,and there is a brief period for warmth or support. At that point, there is the matter of the guardian's unforeseen presentations of fondness as the wellspring of narcissism inside the child. Clearly narrow-minded child rearing can tie the parental presentations of love to the conduct of the child which meets the models of the guardians for progress. That implies that the child just gets warmth gave they play out a specific way or satisfy the desires of the guardians and this sets up the manner in which that they feel friendship ought to be done in their later life.

Fundamentally the object relations devotees consider child narcissism as one of the safeguard reactions or obsessions that are there to child rearing that regards the child as an object intended to legitimize the passionate necessities of the parent as opposed to that of the child since they are the ones that are in require in this correlation. The specific child rearing that outcomes from this narcissistic child rearing can be bantered with an emphasis on extreme control, disregard and conflicting or discontinuous articulations identifying with friendship.

Other researchers argue that childhood narcissism is learned through modeling or reinforcement of the parents.

Particularly, these theorists claim that the parents that tend to indulge the children by allowing their every whim and giving them affection when they want it in spite of their behavior are creating a sense of superiority and entitlement within these children. These are some of the base ingredient s when it comes to narcissism. Such leniency in the parents and non-contingent affection model for the individual as an association between evaluating themselves and performance whereby a positive view of themselves can then exist out of the behavior that they engage. They now see themselves as perfect even if they do something that could be considered reprehensible by the rest of the society. Apparently, the social learning theory is quite opposed to the object relations approach that is suggested by Kernberg. He claims that no parental affection and constant demands for performance can create a state of narcissism through the social learning approach preaches the opposite. The truth though may entail both as they are all forms of abuse that skew the way of thinking of the child for the worse. Rothstein and similar researchers indicted parenting which initiates a contingent link between the behavior and affection.

Empirical considerations

The work done concerning parenting has come up with parenting dimensions that include parental monitoring, warmth and psychological control. These dimensions are there to provide a summary concerning the many parenting components which are connected to child functioning. These elements are the starting blocks for the typologies that are related to the styles of parenting. Attention is set on the individual dimensions related to parenting as the dimensions may predict the particular differences that come in the child outcomes. These predictive impacts can be evaluated when considering the style of parenting.

Monitoring

This is to refer to the way the parent tries to keep track of where the child is and what she is doing at the moment,and it is fundamental as part of the trials of the caregiver to try and make the rules for the child. High levels of monitoring are related potentially to a low level of errant behavior, truancy,and fighting. They are also linked to a high level of academic performance and maturity.

Psychological control

Psychological influence on the children attempts to interfere in their mental and emotional development. It also includes things such as the manipulation of their emotions through guilt or withdrawal and expressions of disappointment and shame within the child. This has been associated severally with behavior deviation and depression and with low self-esteem.

Warmth

This is evaluated under different designations such as child-centeredness, responsiveness,and acceptance. Each of the terms means the extent to the way parents give the emotional and material resources for the infant. The effects of warmth on the way that the child functions are directly related as high levels of warmth are then related with a high level of esteem and sociability. In this vein, a higher level of warmth which is more than necessary even when discipline is needed is what leads to the social learning concept of the origins of narcissism.

Applying parenting theories to the classical theories of narcissism

The dimensions and parenting styles give a logical way through which the clinical theories on narcissism can be tested. Research done by the likes of Kernberg imply that parenting which is high in monitoring and psychological control but low when it comes to warmth is going to predict narcissism during the time of childhood. On the other hand, theories forwarded by Rothstein says that the parents that give a lot of warmth but exercise a lot of psychological control or manipulation will also make a narcissistic child.

Horton, Bleau, Miller, and Campbell have evaluated the three dimensions related to the parenting and the unique association that each of them has had with NPD in children. Inspite of the different parenting measures, it would seem that research done on the parenting narcissism link converges well. The research is discussed while still noting the ways the studies have measured adaptive and maladaptive narcissism.

Adaptive and maladaptive narcissism

The adaptive-ness that relates to different narcissism components can be attributed through the link with self-esteem. Adaptive narcissism refers to scales which correlate positively with self-esteem. Maladaptive narcissism, on the other hand, refers to scale which may link negatively or not with self-esteem. It is significant to note that a lot of studies reviewed are explicit when it comes to their differentiation concerning maladaptive and adaptive narcissism though others are not. Alternatively, maladaptive narcissism evaluates the clinical measures of narcissistic personality disorder such as the personal diagnostic questionnaire.

As such, the links between parenting and narcissism are different as depending on adaptive-ness of narcissism under investigation being investigated.

Evidence for Links Between Child Narcissism and Parenting

Source: https://www.pbs.org/newshour/science/raise-narcissist

Evaluations for the parenting child narcissism link provide consistent support to social learning and object relations. Multiple studies have also found a link between parental indulgence and both the maladaptive and adaptive forms of narcissism. For one, researchers like Watson and parental found that parental submissiveness and permissiveness to be associated with maladaptive narcissism and parental nurturance is positively linked with adaptive narcissism. Otway and Vignoles evaluate parental overvaluation was linked to both adaptive and maladaptive. According to Horton parental warmth was associated positively with adaptive and maladaptive narcissism and parental monitoring corresponded negatively with adaptive narcissism in males. On the overall, parental indulgence and its components are linked consistently linked to the measures of the adaptive and maladaptive narcissism. There is also evidence which points to object relations perspective that narcissism originates from the selfish of the child by the parent.

This is manifested in a lot of parental control. According to Miller, psychological control corresponded positively with maladaptive narcissism when controlling the parenting dimensions. On the overall, the object relations perspective indicting narcissistic control of the child garners a lot of support particularly such as control is linked to the maladaptive as compared to the adaptive parts of narcissism. It should be noted that several of the projects have observed moderating effects of child and parental sex. With regard to the latter, the evidence for the differential influence of paternal or maternal behavior is a bit inconclusive. Where the differences are maternal behavior seems to be strongly linked to child narcissism. Evidence for differential effects of parenting on the male and female children is more convincing. There are already studies which have observed differential effects, and within the main studies, excessive self-control had been positively linked with narcissism only in females. Parental indulgence looks to be linked to narcissism for both female and male participants. Future research should if possible investigate statistical interactions of parenting with child sex and differentiate paternal and maternal behavior.

Chapter 3: Narcissists in Relationships

Narcissists are often perfectionists. In the same vein, nothing done by others is appreciated or right in their eyes. They expect their partners to meet their demands even when they might be unreasonable when it comes to admiration, love or even gifts. The fact that their spouse or partner may not always be able to supply this need because they are sick or busy is inconsequential in their minds. They do not like to hear a negative response to anything that they request,so they expect others to know what their needs are without even asking. They may manipulate things to get their way and they punish, or they make the people who are around them feel guilty just because of turning them down.

In the end, trying to please someone who has narcissism is a thankless task because it can be equated with attempting to fill a bottomless pit. The narcissist also tries and effortlessly manages to get a problem with the efforts of an individual to give service to them considering they are perfectionists and they do not have empathy. So, you may receive backhanded compliments after trying to assist them which would leave you feeling that have not executed the task to completion. If they are pleased for the moment, they are soon asking for more. Unfortunately, when it comes to partner's, they may become, so battle-hardened, the interaction disturbs the way that theyinteract with others. For example, they can often question the sincerity of the narcissist and whether it is just manipulation or a manufactured personality. The partners may feel drained and tense from unpredictable tantrums, false accusations, unjustified indignation and criticism about small or wrongs that were imagined against them. The partners also do not have particular boundaries and absorb anything that is claimed concerning as the main truth.

In a vain attempt to win the approval and stay connected, they can also sacrifice their needs and constantly walk of eggshells for fear of going against the wishes of the easily aggrieved narcissist. They risk blame on a daily basis or being withheld the love that they desire. As such, it would take a deeply insecure individual to put up with a narcissist because they need affirmation on a regular basis and their low self-esteem allows them to constantly seek out the love of the narcissist. Narcissists, in turn, seek out or prey upon these people. The partners have to fit into the cold world of the narcissists and get used to living in a state of emotional abandonment. At any time if they communicate their disappointment, it gets twisted, and it is met with defensive blame or further ways to put them down. The narcissists are very good at gaslighting. They are very good at giving it out, but they cannot take it. Unfortunately, some partners stay because apart from the low self-esteem, narcissists are usually gifted with charm and provide loving gestures that are designed to enchant the partner into returning and staying in line, especially if the narcissist, in this case, senses that there is a breakup in the offing. Now if two of the narcissist's come together, then it is a mismatch because they will fight over the one whose needs should come first. They will also blame and push each other away yet they are miserable as they need each other.

Usually, in these relationships, the narcissists are the ones that give distance when more than sex is anticipated. Getting emotionally close to another individual is a relation toward giving up some of the power and the control. The thought of them being dependent on the other individual is something they absolutely cannot stand as it only limits their options and it makes them feel and appear to be the weak one. Similarly, it also exposes them toward the possibility of rejection and feeling shame which they consciously keep off from all of the time. Their partners who are anxious may chase them and unconsciously replay some of the emotional abandonment from their past.

Stages

Over-evaluation/ Euphoria stage

As stated before, narcissists are very good at selecting those who they would rather bully during the relationships because they have a low self-esteem. This also does not have to be a romantic relationship, as they also practice the same tact when it comes to friendships and other partnerships. Once the target is selected, it is like the narcissist gets a form of tunnel vision. They are quite vigilant when it comes to their pursuit,and they will protect the image that their victim would like them to be. At this time, they would be very caring, attentive and loving as would be expected. They show themselves to be the perfect people in a relationship and they will tend to shower their targets with attention and the right words. They place their targets on a pedestal and worship them. In fact, they are seen to be quite ecstatic and will talk about their targets in a euphoric manner. This will be as close as they get to feeding love to the victim and they will even think they have the same feelings for the person they profess to like.

The victim by this time may be so caught up with all of the attention and is usually thinking at this point they have found their soul mate. The pursuer is exactly what they would anticipate in a partner,and they cannot believe how lucky that this person is still single in the first place.

Devaluation stage

The euphoric phase if you happen tobe dealing with the somatic type of narcissist can last from a few weeks to some months. It is long enough for the narcissist to be confident they have secured the love of the victim and their complete devotion. Unbeknownst to the victim, what was being witnessed in the early part of the relationship was actually the false self of the narcissist. During this second part, the narcissist then reveals their true nature. It could be gradual as they peel back the layers and ease the victim into their true state or it could be sudden.All of a sudden, the attention they had lavished on you in the first place is not there,and it is replaced instead by indifference or silence. In fact, they may be surprised by the way they are acting, but ultimately, they will blame you for it. They may not return phone calls or not keep a promise they had given, and you may then suspect that they moved on to someone else. The victim is mystified and left feeling confusion over what they had done wrong to cause such an about turn. They lose interest with ease because they cannot be engaged by any one person for a long time and what happens in their minds is the void starts to come up again. The high they had initially been feeding off starts to go down, and they start to question how much you are worth to them or whether you are actually useful. It is because they want the void that they have to be constantly gone, so they start to blame you because you are not doing your job of keeping it away as well anymore. Then they become moody and easily agitated and even blame you for the slightest thing that goes wrong. It is at this time they begin to disappear even more frequently, and they will offer silent treatment so that you decide to keep off. On the other hand, you may become their next punching bag because their demands will steadily increase up to the point that you cannot satisfy them anymore and even then, the narcissist will not appreciate the situation.

As the narcissist begins the withdrawal process, their target, due to their personality will most often cling and demand the attention of the former. The harder that the victim may cling to the narcissist the harder they pull away. It is at this time that the target becomes an emotional mess and the narcissist leaves without any explanation. The victim is able to process the extreme between the spectrums of treatment. At one time, they were the most important thing to the other person,andnow the victim has diminished in value to a rate that was previously not fathomable.it is interesting to note the narcissist is a projector,and they tend to project the emotional turmoil onto the person.

They may feed off the misery that others have in the same way that they would feed of the joy that you had given them. It is this duality in their personality that intrigues. They do not like the void that you do not fulfill,and so they enjoy making you suffer for not being able to do it.

The narcissist as such will also not take any responsibility for their actions as they just do not care about the way they have treated the person or how the victim is feeling. That is why the ones who are not familiar with the disorder are just at a loss as the how cruel the behavior of the narcissist can be. The thing is the victim was nothing more than just a target for their use deep down. Taking that into consideration, they are also not just going to throw away a potential supply for their emotional enjoyment. They will keep up the game of hot and cold as long as it suits them or for the duration that you as the victim would endure it. They go in and out of your life as they please and they are quite indifferent to the way that you are suffering. It is quite deliberate at this phase,and one of two things would happen. For one, they might either find a new target or begin the first phase with them,or you may take control and end the cycle which brings in the third phase during a relationship.

Discard phase

Trying to orient oneself after having had a relationship with a narcissist is quite hard. That is because the narcissist usually works very hard to gain the emotional investment of the victim. They make sure the victim gives over to them and is dependent on emotional affirmation just so they can have the option of taking it away when they so,please. As the victim tries to pick up the pieces,thething that needs to be remembered is that they were actually targeted and lied to by someone who is skilled at what they do. There is nothing that the victim should have done differently,and this is usually the hard part to swallow. The narcissist is going to repeat the pattern with every target they successfully woo. As such, allof the former targets must also be vigilantly on guard because the narcissist always reserves the right in their mind to revisit an old source of affirmation provided that person is still weak.

Chapter 4: Narcissism and Attachment Theory

Attachment styles

There are different kinds of attachment patterns,and they include ambivalent, avoidant, disorganized and secure forms of attachment. The securely attached may have trusting and long-term relationships. The other attributes of these kinds of attachment are the individuals may have high esteem and enjoy intimate relationships, seeking social support and an ability to share feelings with others. Then there are avoidant attachment styles where the adults tend to have issues when it comes to relationships and intimacy. These types do not like to invest themselves or emotion in relationships, and they may not experience a lot of distress when there is fallout.

They may avoid intimacy by using excuses, or they could fantasize about others even when they are having relations with their significant others. Research also claims that adults who have such attachment problems tend to accept more, so they are more likely to engage in casual relations. The other common attributes include the fact that they may not support partners at the stressful periods during their life. The disorganized attachment approach in adults is someone that does not often learn healthy manners of soothing themselves. They may also have issues when it comes to socializing and opening up to trusting other individuals. They really tend to struggle in relationships and friendships or during parenting situations. Now the ones with an ambivalent attachment style could be reluctant on becoming closer to other individuals, and they might be worried their partner is not reciprocating the same feelings. This can lead to breakups and usually because there is distance within the relationship.

Relation with attachment styles

Grandiose narcissists for one may experience avoidant attachment patterns in the early parts of their lives, and this has led them to feel they are to take care of themselves. This is the same thought process which leads them to believe they do not need anyone and they ought to be pseudo-independent. Both of the times, the attachment patterns would be created in the adult relationships. During the recent years, research has offered support for connections between the type of narcissism and the style of attachment.

When a child has a caregiver that is a narcissist during the significant years after birth to the age of three then secure attachments may be disrupted. They usually develop avoidant or ambivalent attachment patterns, and these then develop the main core of the relations during the process of their lives. In the rearing years, the children have to obey the agenda of the narcissist parent for their lives to have a semblance of stability. Assertion of emotions, thoughts, and rights may lead to very big issues in the home, and so the children of these types of parents learn that their feelings have no merit in the scheme of things. They usually stifle feelings for peace to be there in the household. When the narcissist parent is being kind, the child learns the kindness has an agenda behind it, and this is often the first time they have a practical orientation to strings attached. The strings may include being favored by the narcissist or being made to feel guilty if they do not perform it to completion. Usually, the parents of the narcissists usually develop insecurity as an attachment style. This is most likely the reason why a child of a narcissist parent would go on to develop ambivalent attachment patterns because their narcissist parents operated hot and cold most of the time. There was no way to predict their pattern, and so there was no way of mapping performance of right behavior with approval or distaste. The child did not have the chance for loving and stable behavior that is needed for the child to have secure attachment patterns.

During adulthood, the individual would have found it hard to stand up to their parents because of their ambivalent style of attachment. They were not validated and so even into the adult years, one finds themselves seeking their approval and validation. This is an unconscious tie that makes them tied to their parents in one manner. As a result of the attachment, the individual, in this case, may prefer that they find a way so they can keep both the partner and their parents within their lives. Of course, the recommendation would be to detach for good from the relationship with the caregivers, but then again, these bonds are very strong.

In the case of the guardians, one would find that narcissists have avoidant attachment style which is not being able to have a relationship or a form of intimacy with a particular individual they should be close to such as their child or a partner or family member. Narcissists have avoidant attachment styles, and a lot of the people that are strongly affected by the narcissists are quite anxious. They have high anxiety type responses to the narcissist's especially when they are devaluing and discarding them. In this case, they are likely to come down with anxiety attacks, and it takes a long time for them to calm down. This would explain the post-traumatic stress response when it comes to the individuals that have abandonment and rejection wounds which have been triggered. An anxious response in having a close relationship being ended all of a sudden is not a laughing matter. The infants for example that experiences disconnect when the primary caregiver is suddenly not there can experience and perceive disconnect as a threat later on. The infant is completely dependent on the caregiver when it comes to food, clothing, and shelter. The ones whose needs are not met on a consistent basis will probably come up with what is known as an anxious or an avoidant anxious attachment to that is directed to the primary caregiver. These attachment styles are then illustrated through the adult romantic relationships.

Not all avoidants are narcissists though they do have the ability to detach themselves from the relationship and this triggers the attachment anxiety from a person. Avoidants are not necessarily comfortable with a lot of closeness which means their relationship dynamic is to push the significant other away so they can initiate a safe distance. The anxious attachment styles that need a lot of closeness with partners can experience being pushed away as reflection or abandonment,and this then triggers deep-seated anxiety. Avoidants may also then find some fault with themselves. As such, in a relationship with this trend, the fingers may be pointed toward the one who is anxious,and this explains why they might feel obligated or the ones responsible at the time the avoidant detach from the relationship. Now when the relations between the anxious and avoidant style end, then the avoidant may easily detach from the relationship and move on where the anxious individual is plagued by the need to reconnect. This need to reconnect tends to be illogical,and it is deeply entrenched as an emotional pattern. The behavior of the avoidant may be abusive and unacceptable though it does not change the need and pull of the anxious person when it comes to reconnection.

There is something that is ingrained in the anxious individual that feels like their survival is dependent on the way that they connect with that individual. The irony that comes with understanding each of these styles is if the anxious or avoidant style gets into a relationship with one who practices secure style of attachment then the anxieties would interestingly be calmed through constant feedback and the anxious individual becomes secure within the relationship.

Even at the time, the relationship comes to an end, the anxious individual is not necessarily triggered when it comes to the way that he or she would be with an avoidant considering there is an open and honest communication where the secure individual shares in the obligation of the relationship. The research studies have illustrated that anxious attachment styles that get into relationships with the ones from the secure attachment orientation have a lot of marital success as compared to two people who have secure attachment patterns.

The problem when it comes to the selection of mates is the avoidant attachment styles are a representation of the largest percentage of single people when it comes to the dating scene. Apparently, this is due to the reason avoidant styles can be afraid of commitment,and so they do not have any qualms severing bonds at the time there is any conflict within the relationship. The avoidant styles,on the other hand, avoid conflict and all relationships at one time or another will have some sort of conflict. As such, there is not going to be a lot of resolution. The issues may tend to be swept under the rug and relationships then break up eventually. If a person is an anxioustype, then the good news is there is a chance of having a healthy relationship,but it would depend on who the partner is. Secure attachment people usually do not come across as the mysterious and charming ones that might be the most attractive. The anxious types may find themselves bored without the conflict or the drama which is initiated by someone who is an avoidant. Trading in intensity for security in a relationship gives the anxious ones, the foundation to develop trust in the ability of their partner to be there consistently.

Going back to this attachment to narcissism, research has considered connections between the vulnerable and grandiose types of narcissists with the attachment styles of the people in their lives or what the latter experienced. Grandiose narcissists have been found to experience avoidant attachment from an early point in their life,andthishave probably made them feel they had to take care of themselves. These attachment patterns are then recreated during the relationships that the narcissists have when they become adults. During the recent years, the research done on this subject has offered connections between narcissism and the styles of attachment.

According to the results from one of the studies, attachment avoidance and attachment anxiety may exert particular influence when it comes to self-enhancement of the part of the narcissists self-enhancement while both attachment anxiety and avoidance foster self-defense.

When it comes to grandiose narcissism, there is research which has found that though avoidant styles are linked to overt forms of narcissism that would include self-praise, attachment anxiety is related to covert forms of narcissism that are then characterized by self-focused attention and an exaggerated sense of being entitled. There are other studies which have also concluded that covert narcissism seems to be related to fearful attachment and the grandiose narcissist approach is better connected to the dismissive attachment approach.

This does not suggest by any means that everyone that experiences insecure attachment styles is destined to become a narcissist though rather the attachment style the narcissist experiences could be very important and give some insight when it comes to treatment even. In exploring this connection, it would be recommended to analyze the characteristics of both covert and grandiose narcissism and how they can be connected to the style of attachment. The covert narcissist preys upon others to increase their self-esteem. They can seek being uplifting and reassurance from other individuals to make them feel okay. They are very good at making things all about themselves as well. The introverted narcissists as well may feel much focused on what they are attaining from other individuals. They go from feeling very superior to inferior according to the ways that others see them or the ways they believe that other individuals may look at them. They come with the attitude that they are nothing if not perfect so to speak. This approach to relating is similar to what is observed with an individual that has a preoccupied attachment approach. Treatment which assists with vulnerable narcissists develops their ability to regulate the emotions they have and develop internal security may allow in the reduction of their narcissist and assist in bringing them to terms with their attachment approach. There was a study that claimed introverted narcissists are linked to interdependent self-esteem while grandiose narcissism is linked apparently to high self-esteem and independent self-construal. As the more typical type of narcissists, they are less likely to consider the way that others think of them and lack empathy for how other individuals are feeling.

There are patterns in the grandiose narcissists that align with the avoidant attachment styles where the individual learned to be reliant on themselves and adapted in feeling so they would not need things from others. They are usually cold towards others and lack any form of compassion. When it comes to those who have an avoidant attachment, it is crucial for them to be in touch with their needs which would allow them to have feeling for the needs of the other individuals. One approach would be to assist in the developing of insight into why they had adopted the style of relating through an exploration of their history on attachment. An approach that would assist in memory access is creating an autobiographical narrative. Exploring the patterns of attachment relates to the expression of narcissism could be through other avenues which can provide information on the manner narcissistic personality comes about and the way that it can be treated.

According to a recent study that was done in 2014, researchers came to the result that assessing the attachment styles in the adults was significant towards understanding pathological narcissism. It is possible that through gaining insight into the attachment history of the individual, it became possible to understand and treat their particular strain of narcissism. In the case of the narcissist, it would also be helpful for them to come to terms with the influence of their history of attachment and so they would have a better chance of understanding themselves and come up with better self-compassion. As such they could challenge their dysfunctional ways when it came to relating to other individuals. This would be executed in the context of therapy and through the process of creating a narrative that is coherent. The analysis of the attachment history and patterns allows individuals that struggle with either form of narcissism a tool that could counter the narcissistic tendencies alienating other individuals and creating distance within the relationships they had.

Chapter 5: How to Spot Narcissists

Narcissists can be quite hard to spot. Over the course of time, they learn the ways to best manipulate their victims,and they get away with their plans without anyone questioning them because they tend to go into situations where they can easily walk out of. What makes it confusing though is they do not all act in the same manner. There are particular patterns of behavior which are consistent though like when they devalue, idealize and discard their romantic partners. The personality of a narcissist is set according to getting their self-esteem requirements met. They may present themselves as secure,but they do have flaws which they do not admit even to themselves. People with these dark triad personalities thrive off of the chaos that is happening in other people's lives, so one of their hobbies is to set up those they are interacting with to fail all of the time. Then they endeavor to punish them the best way they can for failing in the first place. At times, the narcissist may make an empty promise, and then they even get joy out of seeing the reaction of the person when it comes out that they cannot deliver on it. It is a rare form of sadism that thrives on making the other person depend on them so that they control the amount of happiness they have in their life or for a specific period of time. There are some that are so brazen they would even deny making the promise in the first place and gaslight the other person to the point they feel that they are losing their mind.

At times the signs of narcissism may be more nuanced as they are not as obvious as the media would have you think. It is even possible to have some traits of narcissism without having clinically diagnosed narcissistic personality disorder. According to Keith Campbell, a researcher of the disorder, people are on a spectrum, and so there is a range by which to classify individuals.

They currently comprise about 6.2 percent of the population though it usually seems more considering they are usually found within the visible positions of power and leadership apparently. There are various others within the population and this chapter provides a variety of means to detect one and save yourself mental and emotional stress should they decide to make you a target.

Likeability

Narcissists are very good at the first impressions they make on people, and they come across as personable and charismatic. After all, they live their life by preying on emotionally weaker individuals, and so they must first present themselves as God's gift to man so to speak. This is also they tend to perform very well in job interviews. Often times the image that is seen of an individual that is narcissistic at the beginning is very positive, but they tend to not be able to keep the façade on for very long as that also takes a lot of energy to pull off. So, the mask could be sustained for a week or months before their true nature starts to come out. The thing to look out for would be unexpected bursts of rage or anger from the person. They may also uncharacteristically shift moods from happiness to extreme melancholy, anger or indifference. You may also increasingly find that you are to fault for a variety of situations during a small period of time.

Not all are loud

As previously implied there are two forms of narcissism which are relayed in the manner of expression. These are the grandiose approach and the introverted kind. In the grandiose approach, the narcissist uses a bragging approach and shows off a lot while the introverted one shies away from human contact but still has a high opinion of themselves and tend to have a lot of attention issues and feelings of entitlement. The grandiose narcissist is the one often displayed by the media because they are more relatable for human consumption. They make for great entertainment because they are always in others faces and they are quite skilled in manipulation. The introverted kind is the type that sits in a corner and fantasizes when their day will come so that they can take revenge on everyone and resents the success that others have had. That is also not to say that narcissists are either grandiose or shy which are the two possible extremes. In some individuals, there are elements of both the shy and grandiose forms of narcissism apparently. The trouble is people like to classify others in an easily adaptable box though when you observe at how the personality traits present themselves, the separation is only evident at the extreme levels.

Criticism and blaming others

This is one of the more overt features that a narcissist has considering they show their hand by the way they respond to blame or criticism. They are very sensitive to negative emotions and have a very hard time with criticism.

For one to point out the flaws that they have even if it is on a very small matter blows the perception that they have created for everyone else that they are perfect. It also gives a sneak preview of the other personality flaws that they may have, and they cannot stand having people look at them in such a manner. Though, they have zero problems being critical of other individuals and expecting their opinions to be treated not even as truth but as law. They are very talented at making it so that it is the fault of other people but themselves. The best way to spot someone like this would be that they never tend to apologize for anything and you or someone else will be the reason why something did not pan out as it was supposed to in the first place.

Sophisticated Lies

Basically, covert narcissists have a high level of contempt for other individuals and anything that could threaten their level of superiority is made out to be a direct attack. That is the reason they concentrate on being superior and looking down on others. The ones who are above them interms of financial ability or the potential of their careers are supposedly there because they had the benefit of privilege or they were put there by the powers that be. There is always a way to blame the other person, and the fortunes of another are then attributed to something which is external from them. In this way, they might appear to be for the underdog, but it is just to make them seem noble or benevolent. Through supporting the liberal parties or defining themselves as part of the minorities, they would just be tricking people into believing they actually have morals, when their integrity is actually a façade. In this same view, they will tell other lies concerning their parts like the people they have had the chance to associate with or even fictitious job opportunities which they had to turn down because the circumstances were not right or there was an ethical issue. All of it is a lie. In fact, covert narcissists may watch television as they are trying to see what is popular and so they can mimic behavior that they see like empathy. Empathy is used as a good example because it is something which they intrinsically do not have. Escaping from a covert narcissist is hard considering they are very good at draining their victims of energy and resources up to the point that they find the next victim. It is as though when they settle on a victim, they give them an IV drop of poison steadily up to the point that they move on. In fact, their actions are so covered up and misdirecting that one may only know that what they were going through under the clutches of a narcissist is not normal. It is like they woke up from a spell. Hopefully, when they break out of the clutches of someone that is a narcissist, it rings that it was not their fault, so they place healthy boundaries in place to never be the resource of such a person in the future.

They believe that the rules do not apply to them

A narcissist can break the rules of ignoring boundaries as they have a feeling of either entitlement or self-importance which implies they are above everything including the rules set by the society. The narcissist may believe that rules which impede their function are wrong. They are not aware of the bigger picture or,the greater good because it all just about them.

It could be from small things such as interactions with the law to keep off the grass signs. They are intrinsically not able to see why they need to follow these regulations and will make compelling cases in this regard. This is interesting considering they are very likely to make others abide by the very regulations that they would not stand by usually as they live by different standards as the people that are around them. They are however oblivious to the double standards that they place for those who are in their lives.

They like nice things

This is not to say that every shopaholic and materialistic person is a narcissist or that every person with NPD is a shopaholic. However, the hallmark of someone with the condition is the desire to appear that they live a high quality of life and this is shown in their liking for shopping or acquiring items that present them in high status. They may thus do things which are beyond their means like renting a house that is quite expensive or engage in social activities that requirefinances which are above their tax bracket. Their delusions of grandeur make so that they are not aware of reality or their ability to keep up with their preferred status of living. One way to differentiate the common shopaholic from the narcissist is at times the shopaholic will indicate the deal that they got on something to purchase it. Though the narcissist would be more likely to emphasize how expensive something was just to show they could afford it to allude to their high status in life. They will buy a nice car and make sure they quote the price tag to anyone that can listen. One way therefore to spot a narcissist is to look at the way they mention purchases. These are emphasized on the side of the price tag or the location at which it was gotten. It is most likely designer or special edition to show how rare it is. Appearance is therefore quite important to a narcissist. They are not necessarily more good looking than other people, but they make sure that they also take care of their appearance and place a premium on looking very attractive.

Social and financial disasters in their wake

The narcissist tends to have a trail of bad relationships and fallouts behind them which of course are not their fault. When it comes to CEOs that are narcissists, you will see they have gone into firms and destroyed them with delusions of grandeur before moving on to the next project. Companies require nurturing, and investment and this is definitely not the strong suit of a narcissist. They already believe their presence in a company is enough to salvage everything so they will most likely delegate activities to their subordinates but are not intrinsically interested in the way the company is being sustained. In the end, the company may go under,and they will still not be to blame for what is happening as there will always be someone to take that responsibility.

Everything is personal

This is something that would be noted more when it comes to the quieter versions of narcissists. There might not be a sign of over self-promotion or preference to themselves. However, there is defensiveness and a lot of anger if they do not happen to be recognized or if they are able to get their way in so doing. As such, every small slight that happens seems to be a direct affront towards them,and they will claim that accidents were done intentionally even if they were not. They are very sensitive as to the way that others treat them and always make sure they are the individuals that come out at the better end of the deal,and others are suffering. Narcissists may feign sadness if a deal resulted in someone else's loss and their gain but they are internally happy about the result,and it may show if you have been around long enough to notice their tells.

Envy

The narcissist happens to be very envious of others even if they are in a lower position than they are status or situation wise. They also believe concurrently that others are envious of them and what they have. When they see that others are succeeding, it feels like salt in their eyes. They are of the belief that if another person is successful, then it will end up taking away from what they have in terms of success. When they are confronted with bad behavior, they usually rationalize the critic is usually the one who is jealous though they don't want to see the shortcomings in themselves.

Chapter 6: First Steps of Recovery from Narcissistic abuse

With a few exceptions both women and men that have had a relationship with narcissists have had similar thoughts and feelings concerning their partners. They took advantage of them,or they scarred them in a way that they have had trouble getting better from emotionally and mentally. Some of the recoveries has to do with initiation whether you left or were abandoned. When it comes to narcissist relationships, there is a definite victim and a perpetrator whois not the case in normal relationships that can end due to no fault at all. That is the reason the recovery from the narcissist is something else. For one, everything good that you had believed concerning human beings is contradicted. Every thought that was there concerning experience, loyalty, and truthfulness is then denied. Every idea that you had concerning human connection is reversed by the behavior of the narcissist. There are symptoms which show why it is hard to recover from long-term interaction with a narcissist.

Loneliness

Source: https://amicitia.org/the-age-of-loneliness/

Narcissists can try and push other important people away from you to maintain control in your life. They will even keep you away from friends and family. Narcissist family members though may drive away love interests and other friends. Once you decide to break free, it will come to light that you will have to spend a lot of time alone. This is due to bridges being burnt in the process of being with the narcissist.Some of it could be from choice as you try to rediscover yourself and heal from what you have been through. There are other instances that one would want to be social but face the situation where you have gotten rid of all the speed dial contacts,and you may even have become estranged from a few family members. That is why you might decide to cling to the narcissist in the first place because you do not want to be alone and their influence would make you just that if you chose to break away.

Having had your sense of self-identity dismantled by the narcissist during your past, there is a potential for you to face the objective of rebuilding it again once you are alone once more. The process does not only take a significant amount of time though it needs one to face their demons. These would be the remnants of the narcissist's influence within your life. They are the false beliefs about yourself that grew from your experience.

Getting retribution

One of the phases that come during the recovery phase would be the desire for the person to get back at the narcissist that put them there in the first place. It is natural to want them to suffer and to know just how much damage they caused during the whole process spent with them.

Revenge might sound to be appealing premise though each time that you return to the consideration, old wounds are reopened. You begin to stir feelings that were previously not welcome and this result in unwelcome memories which would then push you back a step to a free life. At the same time, this narcissist is a master of manipulation and can see you coming from a mile off. In some way, they may be able to twist the issue so that you could find yourself back in their clutches. Unfortunately, the only way to deal with them is complete disengagement most of the time because they are professionals at twisting the truth or your perception of what is going on especially if they have had a successful track record of doing in the past. The problem is your rational mode of thinking that it is a bad idea, but the emotional centers cannot help but yield to the problem over and over.Many have tried to do it,but they keep coming back to the same situation for this reason.

Questioning yourself

At the time that you decide to separate yourself from this individual, you will also have to face hard questions about yourself from yourself. You will wonder why you did not spot the warning signs early on and this usually happens in the case of romantic relationships. It can be easy for one to blame themselves and then subject themselves to torture for not catching things that now seem to be absolute folly. Of course, everything now happens to be clear in hindsight,butusually, that is not the way that you may see it at this time. As such, you may alternate between the act of forgiving and berating yourself. Each cycle, in this case, may come with its own turmoil. At the same time, you will probably ask the question as to whether you will be able to trust another person with the same intensity that you originally had in this case. The doubt will also make you very pessimistic about anything in that department going forward of course. When you are with the narcissist, it is possible to envision such a life and think that it would be worse than what is happening at that time so you would rather not be alone. Once you are hurt and raw, you may feel like you want to spend a lifetime by yourself and never depend or commit to another person as one would like to. It is also a defense mechanism regardless of the situation, whether it was work, social, familial or romantic relationship. Being able to be self-sufficient allows you to be secure that no one can take advantage of you. Of course, the feeling is not permanent though it can creep back from time to time thus damaging other prospects at connection in the future.

Distancing from Family Members

Rarely, you might find the narcissist is a family member. Considering the solution has been outlined as leaving this destructive person it becomes even trickier to deal with the situation. Family is highly prioritized in a variety of settings in our lives,and when these connections come under threat or are the reason why we are suffering in the first place, then it becomes intensely disheartening. These are individuals that were or have been a part of your life for ages. They may even have been there from the time of birth,and so their influence has helped to shape you to the person that you currently are.

Narcissistic parents are especially challenging considering they are the ones that represent your past and upbringing and how you came into existence. In this case, your bond may not have the same strength as is there when it comes to the traditional parental-child relationship. However, in the same way as one's parents would have, they always have a special place in the heart of a person. The separation that takes place from members of the family does not always happen because they are narcissists. It could be due to serious disagreements that happen which challenge the way that you interact with them going forward. Whatever the reasons may be it is never an easy thing to cut ties with a member of your family especially if they suffer from NPD. You can be guaranteed they will rarely admit they are the ones with a problem and they have a psychological advantage over you especially if they are the elder relative. In this case, the best thing that you can do would be to minimize the points of contact that you have with them. The less number of times that you talk to them or interact, the less influence they have on you and the less number of issues that you will have to sort out later internally. You will have to forego such things like birthdays, funerals and holiday events so that you do not get to see them as often. When it comes to your special events though, this could prove to be hard as the family ties that exist like a wedding or the birth of a child require the unbiased attendance of your family. You may also have a lot of memories which are both good and bad that will enter your mind from time to time,and these will enter your mind on different occasions and become bundled with different emotions that can rise to the surface and confuse you as to the true state of things.

Phases of recovery: implementation schedule

Detachment

When you come to terms that you are dealing with a narcissistic personality, it is advisable to just detach as much as possible from the situation. You need to come from the brink that you are able to salvage the situation and make it better for that particular individual. Truth be told such an individual cannot be changed by their victim,and the only one that you will be able to change in that situation would be yourself. You can do this by refusing to allow continuing to be abused. You deserve to be treated with respect and dignity, and there are times that you need to demand this treatment for yourself. If a person decides to undermine you at every turn and belittle you, then that would mean they do not deserve your time. Unfortunately, the longer that one decides to stay with a narcissist the worse that the treatment gets. There may be a honeymoon period but usually, it just goes back to the way that it was which is them blaming you for everything that goes wrong and it increases with intensity. If you are of the opinion that it is going to change then, you are being delusional. Coming from the fantasy would be the same as coming from the illusion that you have been in the whole time. The illusion has to crumble, and one has to come to terms with the truth.

The first step in detaching is to address the problem and to admit who the narcissist is in your life that has affected it or is currently still drawing emotional energy from you. There are different considerations for the survivor such as the possibility that one has been unconscious to this reality or you may still be in active denial. You may even have unconsciously chosen to ignore the issue and are trying to move from that person. With the varying levels of narcissistic abuse, people may experience and relate to it in some ways.

If you are in such a relationship with such a person or have yet to heal from such an experience, then it is common to want to hide the pain you have experienced from others for fear of shame. It is logical to be a bit unhappy and even to be an expert at hiding and keeping secrets of the difficulties being faced. A survivor of this abuse may have all the signs that they are living a good life and still have the feeling they do not measure up. For some of the survivors seeing through a person's denial may not be done in just one sitting. The fear and the pain at the anticipation of pockets of pain coming to light as they have not yet been processed can be quite daunting and unhealthy. A lot of survivors of narcissistic abuse may seem to be quite strong and component. Internally though, there is a feeling of being untrusting or out of touch with what is safe or what is real. You may have a lot of guilt, depression,and anxiety towards the authority figures. These strong emotions include being angry, passive or even completely submissive or a deep need to be dishonest as a self-preservation mechanism. Such behavior approaches make sense taking into consideration what the survivor had experienced as compared to the narcissist with degrees varying depending on the individual and the circumstances they are in. These mal-adaptive behaviors can be considered,and there is suffering they instigate such as living in fear that you would be found out. You may also chronically avoid the figure of authority.

The first thing to do would be to find a secure approach to expressing emotions that have been bottled up. Take a pen and paper and write about the emotions that you are having trouble with. Emotions like pain sadness, fear and longing are a manifestation of having been subject to a relationship that was making you feel inferior. Once this is done and you have expressed your emotion, you could have cleared some of the ways for trusting in your goodness and worth. This begins by taking a hard look at the value that you hold from a spiritual and practical perspective. It is said that people are spiritual creatures. People are different when compared to non-human forms of life with the ability to reason. The spiritual element which has different names depending on the concept that the person adheres to as with their affiliation is part of an energy that is greater than the human element. It is that mysterious part that would set people apart,and it is understood as a power that is greater than what human beings have to offer. Having a power that is greater than yourself and your affinity for yourself is a great consideration with the level of subservience or feelings or the need to worship any particular person. This reflection can be key to loosening the tie to a narcissist.

You should pause to consider how inherent worth would feel if it was based according to a spiritual truth and not according to beliefs that the narcissist would hope for you to proceed in believing in yourself and the worth of your life.

You can also take time to consider the higher power and questions that you would direct to yourself. You can begin with what may have happened to you at an earlier stage of your life that may have caused you to have low esteem. Many times, low self-esteem is a key tenet for why narcissists chose people so they can prey on them. There may have been a point in time when you had been abused or experienced trauma which lowered your esteem such as abuse from a relative or from a stranger. It may have also given you a deep sense of loss and feeling that every relationship is going to end in the same manner. Bearing this in mind, you might be drawn to believe you do not deserve a happy ending and end up sabotaging healthy relationships and creating ones with people that are not emotionally available or are clearly not the right fit. Some of the people within this category happen to be narcissists. As such a lot of the time, we may think, act and perpetuate the unexamined internal messages that are placed thereto maintain the agenda that they have. In so doing, laying the subconscious cards on the table is one of the significant components when it comes to authentic recovery.

Replacement

The next step that is entailed is the replacement phase. On the first list, jot down attributes that your higher power would not have as they care for you. The second list, you can proceed to place all of the attributes that your higher power would have. In this section, it is okay to be creative, open-mindedas well as, reflective concerning what you envision for this connection. Upon finishing, there may be patterns that come out between the two lists. For example, you might see that the attributes which were listed in the negative column were instances you were hurt. It could be that you are still being hurt in these ways either from yourself or from another person (narcissist). When it comes to the positive column, you might notice you are deeply touched by these attributes because you either have them yourself, or others have them. You may see that on the negative list, the attributes are very similar to that of the narcissist. When you see the positive list, a new concept may start to review and might be unlike the old archaic one. You may begin to feel a sense of hope and courage so that you start the process of recovery from this toxic relationship. Hopefully, you will be able to glean your good features and at least start to come to terms that you are a good person. From there, you can start to assume the possibility of being able to exist as an entity by yourself guided by your higher power. It is not an easy process in the least, but it is quite necessary if a person is to succeed from being enslaved as part of the emotional resources of another person.

Chapter 7: Moving on from Narcissistic Abuse

At the end of a toxic relationship, it would become quite easy for one to remain in the past and this is the same whether the narcissist in question is family member, friend, or romantic connection. You typically find yourself asking questions such as what you would have said or done in a different mannerto avoid that one last fight and end up assigning part of the blame to yourself. As such, now that you are free from the narcissistic and their cycle of abuse, you need to continue with your life so as not to be sucked back into their gravitational pull. That being said there are different elements which are involved when it comes to moving on from narcissistic abuse. In the same case with any loss, there will be a lot of grieving, anger,and depression. In this case, you would need to get to a point of acceptance and avoid any unnecessary fixation on the situation.

Allow yourself time to grieve

Many of the victims that suffer from narcissistic abuse have the wrong perspective that since the partner was nottruthful, the relationship was one-sided,so there is nothing to grieve if it was all a lie. Not allowing yourself to come to terms with the feelings that come from the end of the interaction usually leads to detrimental results at a later time like getting stuck on an emotional and mental level. This can result in repressed feelings of anger and sadness. You may also experience prolonged exhaustion or indifference to things that should cause an effect. You may take addictions such as pills or alcoholism as a means of escape from the emotional situation within yourself.

Learn ground or self-soothing

You need to learn methods that would ground you that only apply to your case or that which you are comfortable utilizing. They work in different scenarios from anger, to anxiety attacks and even addictions. There is a lot that you can do in the name of self-soothing which would assist in dampening the emotional hijacking that happens severally when a person is going through these issues. The best approaches are the same which are coincidentally used to deal with PTSD triggers and emotional trauma. This could be everyday activities which have been readapted by the individual, so they are able to deal with certain situations. It almost has a hypnotic effect on them. They may include driving, counting up to ten or even just taking successive deep breaths. The activities are meant to bring the emotional distress of the person down to manageable levels especially when they fell like breaking down. Learning self-soothing is a significant step because any activities that one would engage in to heal and move on would be continuously attacked by the emotional triggers up to a point that the individual caves into their state.

Get professional assistance if you are damaged

Complicated forms of grief are long lasting and can be hard to get over especially if it entails mourning the damage that had been done to your psyche. This is quite common in the aftermath of abusive relationships because the victims are not allowed the validation they had wanted in the first place,and they do not get what amounts to closure. After the end of a relationship which has been abusive, there is a lot of unfinished business such as disputes which have not been settled and discrediting of the character of an individual not to mention questions which are unanswered about unrequited love. As the victim, one is left hanging and unable to complete the relationship that you have with the narcissist. In this case, there are elements within your psyche that are unaccounted for, and these elements require one to seek professional help for you to truly heal. For example, severe cases of emotional trauma cannot be managed by self-soothing alone. They need to be uncovered, and you would have to go through a whole guiding process with a counselor so that you could heal. If left untreated, these wounds tend to fester and create problems for you and others you will interact with in the future. It may even be necessary depending on the instructions as issued by the counselor to go on medication. However, it would also be pertinent to opt for the ones which do not give addictions, i.e., opiate free.

Do not obsess

When you have been abused in such a manner by a narcissist, it can be jarring because it seems so diabolical. You also want to get to the bottom of the situation and figure what happened between the two of you or why the person acts in the manner that they do. During the phase of recovery educating yourself concerning narcissism is crucial when it comes to understanding how the disorder works and it also assists you to come to terms with the dynamics of a relationship with a narcissist. On the other hand, when it is time to heal; your focus should be on the appropriate healing methods and self-care in the long run. Constant research done on the attributes of the disordered person becomes counterproductive,and you become drawn to them as opposed to your healing proves. Each time that you repeat a thought or an action then it becomes reinforced as a connection between your neurons. This turns those thoughts into a way of life which influences your reality from day to day. The implementation of self-care patterns which are positive and healthy could be a bit hard at first because it is counter-intuitive.With a lot of practice and intentional consideration with time, they also become habitual,and they will assist in the recovery process.

Self-esteem work out

The one thing you need to realize is the perceived rejection that came about from the narcissist in question is an illusion. This can be quite hard to do considering your emotions will be screaming a thousand different things. You will feel shame and rejection on a level which is hard to deal with if you are not strong. But you need to realize their goal is just that to make you feel as inconsequential as possible and invisible.

What that means is even if they secretly perceive that you are attractive or even successful or the best partner they have ever been with, they would rather be in physical pain than to admit it unless it was of benefit in the process to further manipulate you. Narcissists strive to take away the most of your self-esteem because that is the only way they can keep you wanting for more of their attention. You will want to attend them and possibly fix them. They will also have you thinking that it is great that you at least have someone around than no one at all. The fact that someone treats you like garbage is beside the issue while it ought to be the most important aspect of the equation. You have to also rememberthat most of what they claim is a lie so their perspective should be the one that is invalid.

Emotional Freedom Technique

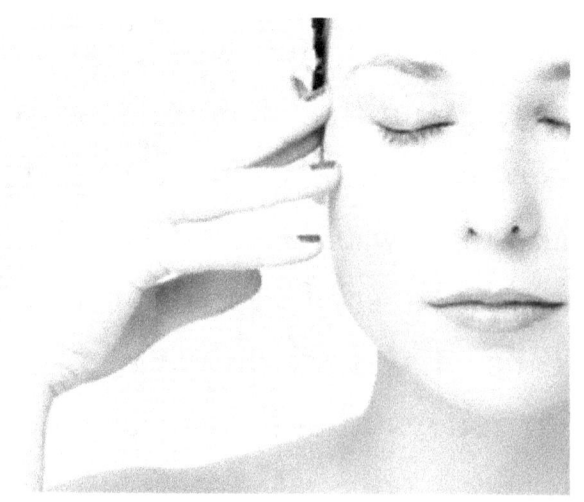

Source: http://newyork.carpediem.cd/events/75 65195-emotional-freedom-technique-tapping-workshop-at-aquarianyoga-center/

Emotional freedom technique or the EFT was initiated by an engineer known as Gary Craig who considered some acupressure methods for healing even though he did not have any training in psychology. The problem with these approaches is they utilized complicated arrangements on the acupuncture points. Craig came up with a simplistic formula that entailed tapping on some acupressure of acupuncture points while still focusing on the issue at hand. The EFT system has been found to be incredibly effective for some issues from anxiety to depression to even phobias and physical illness. As such, it has also been effective with issues to do with trauma from narcissistic abuse.

The acupressure points that are used in EFT come from Traditional Chinese Medicine as concerns a system of healing that has been developed over the course of several thousand years through trial and error. Gary Craig developed the original EFT formula and the tapping so he could approach it from a spiritual perspective that is known as the 'Unseen therapist.' The EFT model assists victims of narcissistic abuse in a variety of ways. Using EFT would make a difference as concerns anxiety, depression and stress. When it comes to Traditional Chinese Medicine, negative emotions come from blocked energy in what is referred to as the meridian channels. The tapping that is exercised in EFT stimulates new energy or chi to flow,and it removes things which would be an emotional blockage. EFT can also help with the lowering of cortisol levels. At the time the energy begins to flow then it would be helpful in the reduction of cortisol that is also referred to as a stress hormone that can be an issue when too much of it is produced. Cortisol is thus in plenty when you are recovering from narcissistic abuse and EFT would be useful in the reduction of these levels. NPD abuse can also lead to nightmares, phobias and panic attacks all of which are side effects of the relationship. Fortunately, these symptoms are very responsive to EFT treatment. You might have to come at the issue from different angles before getting full relief. In the severe scenarios entailing PTSD caused by EFT, you may consider going to an EFT practitioner that is licensed or a licensed therapist.

EFT is effective also in dealing with childhood wounds which often times lead to low self-esteem. Sometimes it is a bit hard to get over these issues that arise from past trauma,and this is what a narcissist would exploit for their gain in the future. Through working through these old wounds, you would be securing your mind and making yourself impervious to the charms of a narcissist. To heal from narcissistic abuse, you should have the expectation that you are going to need multiple sessions from EFT. Though the model can assist with some problems almost instantly, when it comes to the deeply set issues there may be a need to work on multiple layers. If EFT is not effective after tapping on one element then you can try another one. Let's say if you were in a fire and you tapped on the fear,and it only helped a little. Through tapping on another subject concerning the scenario which is more specific like the feeling of the heat on your skin you may have come closer to the problem.

Chapter 8: Emotional Self-Care Practices forNarcissistic Abuse Recovery

When survivors of emotional abuse leave the harmful relationship, they have just begun on their journey of healing. In fact, it becomes a lifestyle in which you have to practice so as not to back-peddle to the position that you were in the first place when the interaction between you and the narcissist ended. Victims of psychological abuse continuously have symptoms of trauma such as nightmares, recurring flashbacks,and anxiety.

They also have depression and feelings of low self-esteem. They could even have an urge to check or even connect with their abuser because of the intense trauma bonds which are there during the abuse cycle.

Gradual practices of self-care to supplement the therapy that you should get after detachment are some of the powerful ways to tend to the mind, body,and spirit after being abused. Though not every healing approach would work for every survivor, experimenting with these practices and finding the ones which suit your scenario would be advantageous.

Eat healthy and keep a healthy mental status

In this busy world, people often do not have time to have a proper meal and sometimes does it while doing work or watching television. In so doing, they deny themselves the pure experience of a meal which is nourishing and well thought out. You need to treat yourself with the same respect that you would give a first date and so indulge yourself to a meal without having a lot of distractions as well. That means having the right proportion for each food group in your meal such as protein, vegetables,and starch. When your diet is right then, you will have the right energy levels and be more likely to be as mentally strong. During the times when the brain is traumatized, the areas of the brain that relate to executive functioning, emotion and focus become disrupted. Meditation has actually been proven from a scientific basis to benefit similar parts of the brain which have also been affected by trauma like the amygdala, the hippocampus and the prefrontal part of the cortex. That is because meditation entails clearing your mind completely of things which burden you and allowing you to process things which have burdened your subconscious for a long time. In so doing, you will find you are no longer guided by your emotions,but you are placed back in the driving seat of your psyche. It enables the survivor,so they are able to claim their reality and act from an area of empowerment as opposed to a place designed by the trauma. You can develop daily meditation practices assists in the strengthening of neural pathways in positive ways, which increases grey matter density in parts of the brain that are related to regulation of emotion and it also mitigates the way that a person would respond to fight or flight response which may destabilize after one goes through trauma include narcissistic abuse. Therefore, meditation allows you to be in better control of the way that you would respond to trauma triggers. Meditation apparently also enables one to be aware of your cravings so that you do not cave in and start to contact the narcissist who will take this as a sign they will be able to continue with their abuse. It would allow you the spaceto consider the potential alternatives before deciding to act impulsively on urges to go back to the interaction.

Exercise

This is not only for the physical benefits that translate into mental health; it is also for the advantage of discipline. Exercising on a regular basis can make you better able to handle your emotions because the act itself instills discipline in your psyche. A daily exercise regimen can save your life after being abused.

It could be running on the treadmill or even going to aerobics classes or long walks. If you do not have the motivation, then you just have to set yourself up with something that you enjoy. This could even be thirty minutes of walking each day or an hour if you feel that it is necessary. The reason is exercise tends to release endorphins and lowers the levels of cortisol which then replaces the biochemical addiction that is developed with the abusers with a healthier outlet.

Exercise may allow the individual to embody increasing resilience and strength after getting free from a narcissist. It combats the biochemical addiction that the body developed during the abuse. This addiction is created through the release of chemicals such as adrenaline, cortisol serotonin and dopamine which exaggerate the bond that one has with their abusers through the highs and the lows that are there during the abuse cycle. The benefit of exercise is that it can counter the physical side effects which are there with the abuse such as gaining weight, prematurely aging and illness which are all caused by an immune system which is being overwhelmed by stress from trauma. Stress does limit the ability of the immune system to counter diseases,and narcissistic abuse can cause the immune system to be weak to a point of exaggerating illness or allowing infections to take hold.

Taking care of your inner child

Even though you may have been traumatized, there could have been other instances which were brought to the surface because of the abusive relationship. Your id may be wounded and thus would need to be soothed by your adult self when you are feeling emotional. The unmet needs during childhood were probably compounded by the experience which means self-compassion is needed during this time. Survivors tend to struggle a lot with blame and shame after their abuse. Even though they are aware, the abuse was not their fault. It has the power to bring up old issues which were not addressed. It may also point out to a larger pattern of not being good enough. Changing the course of your negativity is crucial when one is healing as it assists in tackling narratives which were mostly cemented because of the new trauma. At the time that these deep-seated emotions arrive, you have to be gentle with yourself as if you were actually speaking to someone that you love. You can proceed to write down positive words of affirmation whenever you feel overwhelmed by the feelings of grief. Remember when you are blaming or judging yourself, you have a higher likelihood of engaging in self-sabotage because you do not feel that you are worthy of peace and stability. When you finally accept and show love for yourself, you will remind yourself that you are worthy of your own care and kindness.

Reality check anchoring

This allows for the habit of reconnection with reality to take place as it is something that the abuser had eroded at first. It validates the survivor,and it reduces dissonance concerning the identity of the narcissist. Survivors may be very vulnerable after leaving the abusers,and the latter usually try and manipulate them into going back to their routine.

That is why it is necessary to not only block texts and calls from your abuser but also remove connections between them and other enablers that are on social media. That would remove temptation and information on the narcissists from the healing journey. It would also provide a clean slate where one can reconnect with what really happened and the way that it made you feel or how the narcissist will try to manipulate the situation going forward.

Conclusion

Narcissism has been around for a long time, but it is only recently being given the attention that it deserves as concerns recovery from such abuse. Narcissus was the first indication in the history of a person that was in love with themselves to the extent they wanted to have a romantic relationship with their reflection. This book considers the history and theories of narcissism before elaborating on narcissistic abuse and the means that a person can use to recover from such treatment. There are different approaches as to why narcissism starts in individuals from the time of childhood. These would be the object relations and social learning constructs. In the former case, the individual is nurtured in an environment where the caregivers are quite harsh on everything that they do. The person has no choice but to develop perfectionist tendencies that end up being used for relationships. They also develop a disparaging attitude towards others and measure human value according to their standards. The theory appears to be counter-intuitive, but it results in the same thing which is someone that only considers relationships as a means to an end. The social learning theory considers the entitlement side of narcissists whereby caregivers allow the narcissist to do anything they please during the formative years. In this way, they feel they can get away with anything, and this translates into their worldview as they grow up. It is no wonder that during relationships they feel a certain sense of entitlement and take advantage of people that have a low self-perception. The book also dispels some myths about narcissist such as the one that they are internally hurting and think very lowly of themselves which is why they manipulate to get what they want.

It is not hard to see why this theory is furthered. After all, they have tendencies such as envy and manipulation which are both traits that you would expect to see in a person that has low self-esteem. They are not insecure about their status or their appearance. Quite the opposite in fact, as they have a high self-esteem and think the world revolves around what they do and what they think. Some narcissists would be described as introverts. This group of narcissists also displays the same tendencies of entitlement and self-regard that the aggressive narcissists have. The net part of the book deals with the types of approaches that narcissists use to be prepared for their advances and avoid the abuse that will follow thereafter. This includes the phases of an interaction with a narcissist.

At first, there is a feeling of euphoria that they bring to the interaction. It is like they are too good to be true and they are. They make it very easy to trust them and to make them the center of your world. Because the façade takes a lot of energy to keep up, it can only last for a short time such as weeks or months at most before they snap. This is the beginning of the cycle of abuse that you would be subjected to. The abuse has a cyclical nature. At one time, it would seem the person is emotionally feeding on your fears, shame,and ambition and the next thing is you are suddenly uplifted and become important again. By this time, they will have broken your psyche down so that you are a slave to what they think and say about you. In fact, there are cases where the person's emotional health is so damaged they feel to see any abuse going on,but it is evident in the rest of the world. The narcissist is also intelligent to the point they start to isolate you from others because they know that for the abuse to work uninterrupted, you should not be affirmed by the likes of friends and family that would reinforce your mental and emotional strengths. That also lends to the reason why it is so hard to get over narcissistic abuse.

The first thing is you have to accept there is a problem and the problem is a particular person. The second thing is to admit that you have a problem and that is the reason that you are still in the relationship with that particular person. Going forward the book considers different approaches that you can take to sever the connection with the narcissist and then make sure the connection is cut because narcissists keep trying to contact their prey even after they have fallen out. The recovery process seems a bit counter-intuitive, but it is necessary if it is to work. During a relationship with a narcissist, they make sure to break down your patterns of thought to fit what they feel is suitable and they make it so that they want what is best for you. In the end, it becomes baffling as to how they were able to do so much to your emotional health and the harder question is what motivated them to do such a thing to someone. That is why recovery entails breaking away from the person and steering clear of that person rather than trying to figure out what went wrong. Detachment is better than obsessing and falling back into a cycle which is comparable to addiction. As such, the best way to consider the narcissist is the same way that one would look at cocaine or a predator. The only way forward is to avoid them. Narcissist'srelationships operate in such a manner there is a predator and a victim. This is applicable regardless of the interaction between the individuals which can be work-related, social, romantic or transactional. The narcissist views others as potential prey or insignificant in the grand scheme of things.

The recovery methods used for narcissistic abuse would be said to be similar to the ones that are used for recovery from post-traumatic stress. It is that bad. As the victim, you are prone to having anxiety attacks or breakdowns once you think about the past interactions. Some of these recovery approaches include EFT which is a way to reduce levels of cortisol, adrenaline and other PTSD symptoms. It also assists in helping with physical manifestations of pain related to narcissistic abuse.

During the time that you had been in the relationship with this person, they separated you from friends and family or tried to limit the connections that you had with the outside forces. It is quite daunting,but after breaking up or severing connection with such a person, it would be advisable to recreate the bonds that you had with particular people in your life that you had lost touch with. This will help with any feelings of obsession or loneliness when you detach from the abuse. There is a void that is left over after the breakup,and this needs to be filled with something constructive. Otherwise you may fall back to destructive behaviors.

That being said you also need to grieve for your sake. Many are of the perception that if the relationship was a fraud, then it would be pointless to grieve as if the act is giving something to the perpetrator,but this is not the case at all. The purpose of grieving is for you because you would be grieving your feelings which were taken advantage. The grief is for your mind and emotional health and from there; you can take part in some self-healing approaches which will take you further along the path of recovery. Some of these approaches include exercising and keeping a healthy mental status. Exercising allows your mind to keep fit as well as your physical state. The purpose of working out is also to create a sense of mental discipline which will then instruct your thought process and make you less vulnerable to narcissistic abuse in the future. There is also self-soothing and anchoring which is similar as they tie you down to reality. These activities are meant to give you a sense of security in your thought process and the relationships that you have with other people. Self-reassurance acts as the optimal guidance system. It makes you sure of yourself and assists in the overall healing process. Recovery from narcissistic abuse takes time and ought to be adopted as a lifestyle because it is meant to rewire the way that you perceive relationships and yourself.

www.ingramcontent.com/pod-product-compliance
Lightning Source LLC
Chambersburg PA
CBHW071242070526
44583CB00017B/2297